DANGEROUS D[INOSAURS]

by **Adam Hibb**[ert]

Contents

Clever Clogs Books
Copyright © 2006 *ticktock* Entertainment Ltd.
http://www.ticktock.co.uk

TERRIBLE LIZARDS

Dinosaurs roamed the world for 145 million years, before suddenly dying out about 65 million years ago — long before humans were around. From huge treetop-nibbling plant-eaters, to chicken-sized hunter-killers, dinosaurs in all shapes and sizes reigned as the supreme land animals.

Tyrannosarus rex scavenging

SUITS YOU, SIR!

Dinosaurs were scaly, but skin doesn't survive in fossils, so we can only guess their colours!

DINO'S DOMAIN

Dinosaurs first appeared around 210 million years ago, when all the world's dry land was still one continent, Pangaea. There were huge deserts inland where nothing could survive. But as Pangaea began to split into pieces, the climate turned moist and warm, and every part of the world became dinosaur heaven!

HERE BE DRAGONS

Before modern science, people made sense of dinosaur fossils through religion. In China, the fossils were thought to belong to dragons, and the teeth were used for magic potions. Canadian Blackfoot Indians thought that they were the bones of a sacred buffalo ancestor. In Europe, Christians believed they were the bones of strange animals, drowned in the biblical flood.

DINO QUIZ

When did South America, Africa and India split apart?

a) 80 million years ago
b) 100 million years ago
c) 120 million years ago

What is a fossil?

a) a dead body
b) a bone
c) a bone that has turned to stone

Which of these continents has no dinosaur fossils?

a) Australia
b) South America
c) Antartica

(answers on page 32)

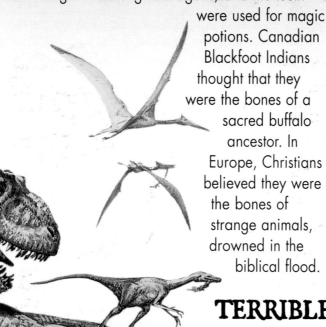

TERRIBLE NEWS

It was only around 150 years ago that scientists realised a whole world of fantastic animals had existed before humans. This news promised a revolution in biology. In 1841, the scientist Richard Owen named the animals dinosaurs, meaning 'terrible lizards'.

NICE LEGS

The scientific definition of a dinosaur is a reptile with tucked-in legs. Dinosaurs are the only reptiles to have developed legs like this which can carry great weight or support an upright posture.

BEARDY OLD BRACHIOSAURUS

Even if you eat trees, it takes time to get this big. *Brachiosaurus* might have lived to be 125!

DINO QUIZ

How heavy is the biggest dinosaur bone?

a) 122 kg
b) 301 kg
c) 675 kg

How big was the biggest dinosaur egg?

a) 3 x the length of a chicken's egg
b) 5 x the length of a chicken's egg
c) 15 x the length of a chicken's egg

How long was the longest dino neck?

a) 5 metres
b) 7.5 metres
c) 10 metres

(answers on page 32)

TOP TIP

Ankylosaurs weren't very long (up to a mere 5 metres!), but they were heavy and rather slow. They had thick armour on their backs, and lay flat on the ground when attacked. Predators had to try to tip them over to reach their soft bellies, but it wasn't easy!

THE EARTH TREMBLED!

Sauropods could rear up on their hind legs to nibble at treetops. One sauropod skeleton in a New York museum reaches 17 metres high (that's the height of three giraffes!). Some bones of an even bigger sauropod than *Brachiosaurus* have since been discovered. Scientists have nicknamed their unknown owner *Seismosaurus*, or 'earth-shaking lizard'.

GINORMOUSAURUS!

Ankylosaurus

Scientists can't agree on whether dinosaurs were cold-blooded, like reptiles, or warm-blooded, like birds and mammals. But they know that big animals don't have to worry about temperature changes as much as little animals. Perhaps that's why some dinosaurs grew so big – and some were very big indeed!

STUPENDOUS SAUROPODS

The biggest land animals to ever exist were a group of plant-eating dinosaurs called sauropods. One sauropod, *Brachiosaurus*, was 12.5 metres tall, 23 metres long, and weighed between 45 and 75 tonnes (as much as 9-15 large elephants!).

Brachiosaurus

BATHING BEAUTY

Despite being as long as five elephants, some sauropods could move quite daintily. By studying fossilised footprints in what was once a shallow lake in Texas, scientists who study fossils (called palaeontologists) have discovered that sauropods went paddling! They floated along using their front feet to tiptoe along the bottom.

KING LIZARD

When palaeontologists began to uncover a dinosaur skull in Montana, USA, in 1902, they could hardly believe what they were seeing. Emerging from the 70-million-year-old rock was the unmistakably toothy grin of the most fearsome predator ever to have stalked the earth – *Tyrannosaurus rex!*

NOT ENTIRELY ARMLESS!

The *Tyrannosaurus rex* had such effective biting equipment that it seems to have stopped using its forearms as weapons; they became tiny, and were probably only ever used to help it stand up after a nap. But no fossil *T-rex* has yet been found with a complete claw (museums use *Albertosaurus* claws instead), so the mystery continues.

Tyrannosaurus rex skull and upper skeleton

GREAT PRETENDER

There are clues to suggest a challenger to *T-rex's* position as the supreme meat-eater. Only the arms and 'hands' of a newly-discovered species, *Deinocheirus*, have been found so far. Each arm is longer than a grown man. If *Deinocheirus* was built to the same shape as *T-rex*, this would make it almost twice as big!

DENTAL DISASTER

With a diet of raw and rotting flesh, *T-rex* probably had a king-sized bad breath problem!

Scene from Jurassic Park

When did tyrannosauruses rule the world?

a) 120-170 million years ago
b) 5 million years ago
c) they're still out there!

What should you do if you see a tyrannosaurus running towards you?

a) cross your legs
b) give it a friendly wave
c) keep eating your popcorn

How long was the tyrannosaurus' 'smile'?

a) 1 metre
b) nearly 2 metres
c) 5 metres

(answers on page 32)

KING OF THE KILLERS

Looming out of the jungle mists, the *T-rex* was 14 metres of muscle, claw and tooth. Standing erect, it was as tall as three grizzly bears, and probably hungrier! Its mouth was lined with serrated-edge teeth like 15-cm steak knives, and could open wide enough to swallow a 12-year-old human in one gulp!

LOUNGE LIZARD?

Some people think the *T-rex* was too big and sluggish to run after its own prey. They suggest that it relied on scaring other, niftier predators away from a kill. Other people think that it approached prey by stealth, and pounced. Study of fossil footprints suggests that *T-rex* walked at about human speed, roughly 5km/h.

SMALL BUT DEADLY

The ferocious *Deinonychus* was 3 metres long from the tip of its nose to the end of its tail, but its head would only reach a man's shoulder, and it weighed a mere 75 kg. Like its larger cousin, *Velociraptor*, *Deinonychus* must have made up for its size by its intelligence and its quick responses.

DINO QUIZ

When did *Deinonychus* first appear?

a) 140 million years ago
b) 100 million years ago
c) 65 million years ago

Why are so many dino remains found in the wilds of Montana, USA?

a) they got bored of city life
b) they made nests in the hills
c) they liked to go hiking

How do we know which dinos ate meat?

a) they lived longer
b) they were fatter
c) by the shape of their teeth

(answers on page 32)

Megalosaurus tooth

FANG MONSTER

Most meat-eaters (carnivores) weren't equipped with such amazing claws, but they made up for it by having terrible teeth instead! *Megalosaurus* had two special fangs jutting from its lower jaw. Each of them was nearly 20 cm long, with a saw-edge for ripping through meat.

CLAWS OF DEATH

Scientists once argued that dinosaurs must have been cold-blooded, sluggish, and probably a bit stupid. But in 1964, a terrible new predator was unearthed in Montana, USA, which gave everyone a shock. It was the small, speedy, big-brained and obviously vicious *Deinonychus*, or 'terrible claw'.

Deinonychus

LICENCE TO KILL

Deinonychus was designed for pursuit, with a large but very light skull. Its 'terrible claw' was a 12-cm 'flick knife' in a sheath on powerful rear feet. A kick from this deadly weapon could slice open the belly of large prey, causing it to collapse to the ground; *Deinonychus* could then go to work with its razor-sharp teeth.

FANCY A HUG?

Deinonychus also had unusually well developed arms and wrists, similar to humans in the number of ways they could move. The arms ended in more claws. For difficult prey, *Deinonychus* may have jumped into the air to 'hug' a large plant-eater (herbivore) with its arms. It could then slash with its hind legs, like a modern-day kangaroo.

KEEP'EM KEEN

Deinonychus took great care of its deadly claws, keeping them razor-sharp.

9

HUNTING IN PACKS

Scientists were very excited to discover that *Deinonychus* might have been a social hunter, roaming the prehistoric landscape in family packs, in much the same way as lions and wolves do today.

Triceratops

It meant that several other small meat-eaters already known about might not just be scavengers, but active predators.

RUN FOR IT! If you can't fight, run! *Dromiceiomimus* escaped its enemies at speeds of up to 60 km/h.

HIGH JINKS

By working as a team, *Deinonychus* could have charged into herds of heavy, plant-eating dinosaurs, singling out the young and weak for an easy meal. But they would also have caught quite agile prey; their tails were specially-made for flicking sideways, letting them 'jink' around tight corners at high speed.

CANNY KILLERS

Hunting socially takes brains! Dinosaurs that worked together would need to be able to communicate with each other (as wolves do today, for example), and might have set up sophisticated ambushes for their prey. If they were truly this crafty, they would be cleverer than any reptile alive today.

WALL OF FEAR

If plant-eaters (herbivores)had to defend themselves from packs of meat-eaters, they may have responded as elephants do today. If so, the adults would have put themselves between their babies and the predator, forming a formidable barrier. Even the hungriest *Velociraptor* must have been afraid of a wall of *Triceratops*, with their fearsome horns.

SPEED DEMON

Velociraptor, the swift hunter, was discovered in Mongolia in 1921. But it was only after discovering its cousin, *Deinonychus,* that scientists realised such animals might have hunted in packs. *Velociraptor* could easily have run down and killed much bigger dinosaurs if it had worked as a group.

DINO QUIZ

What did the *Ornithomimid* look like?

a) a beetle
b) an ostrich
c) a possum

Working together would allow pack hunters to eat animals...

a) twice their size
b) 5 times their size
c) 10 times their size

How do we know that *Triceratops* lived in herds?

a) from their birth certificates
b) fossilised footprints
c) we don't really know

(answers on page 32)

Jurassic Park: The Lost World

MURDEROUS MEAT-EATERS

DINO QUIZ

How long ago did *Allosaurus* live and hunt?

a) 210 million years ago
b) 150 million years ago
c) 70 million years ago

Why did the 74 teeth of *Allosaurus* curve backwards?

a) to stop it biting its lip
b) for better grip on prey
c) there were no dinosaur dentists

When was the first big meat-eating dino described by a scientist?

a) 1824
b) 1845
c) 1902

(answers on page 32)

Life for meat-eating dinosaurs could be tough – if they wanted dinner, first they had to hunt down and kill it! But *Tyrannosaurus rex* and its close relatives were the best hunters the world has ever known.

CHILD-KILLER!

Coelophysis, an early meat-eater, was an especially nasty customer, if an unusual *Coelophysis* fossil from Texas is anything to go by. Just where its belly would have been, scientists found the bones of several *Coelophysis* babies – so this dinosaur was a cannibal.

D'YOUTHINKESAURUS?

Allosaurus had fantastic eyesight. Despite being slightly smaller than *Tyrannosaurus rex*, its eyes were twice as big, which would have helped it hunt at dawn or dusk. *Allosaurus* had bony ridges over the eye socket – probably to shield its eyes from the sun.

Allosaurus

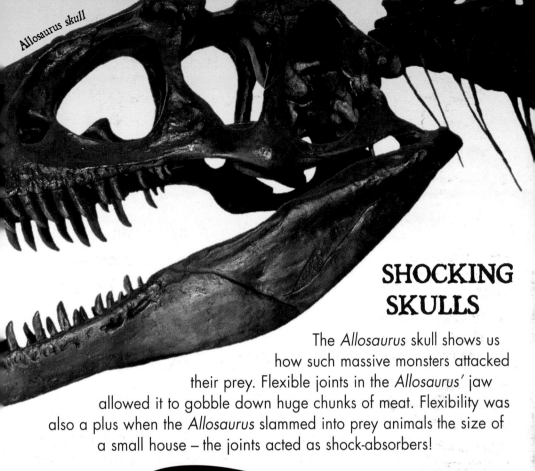

Allosaurus skull

SHOCKING SKULLS

The *Allosaurus* skull shows us how such massive monsters attacked their prey. Flexible joints in the *Allosaurus'* jaw allowed it to gobble down huge chunks of meat. Flexibility was also a plus when the *Allosaurus* slammed into prey animals the size of a small house – the joints acted as shock-absorbers!

ROCKS FOR DINNER

Some dinosaurs made up for their lack of chewing teeth by swallowing rocks. The rocks ground around in the dinosaur's stomach, chewing the meat for it.

BALANCING ACT

What all the hunters had in common was a big head! *Allosaurus'* skull is 1 metre long, and *T-rex's* is even bigger. Stretching their huge heads forward as they burst from the trees towards their prey, these dinosaurs would all have toppled over without their heavy tails to balance them.

TERROR IN THE SKY

Pterosaurs (pronounced without the 'p') weren't proper dinosaurs, but they were still quite big and scary.

Rhamphorhynchus

They dominated the skies before birds and bats arrived on the scene. Although they were reptiles, with big flaps of skin instead of feathery wings, most of them lived as modern birds do.

CLEAR THE RUNWAY!

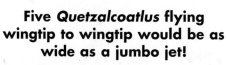

Five *Quetzalcoatlus* flying wingtip to wingtip would be as wide as a jumbo jet!

PTRULY PTERRIBLE

The really big pterosaurs didn't appear until about 150 million years ago. *Pteranodon* was a tailless monster with a big, bony crest behind its skull. It lived a life similar to today's albatross, gliding above the waves. The recently discovered *Quetzalcoatlus* had a wingspan of up to 15 metres!

FIRST FLAMINGO?

One pterosaur managed to beat the flamingo to the art of shrimp-fishing! Millions of years before flamingos existed, *Pterodaustro* was equipped with a very bristly bottom jaw, which it would have used like a sieve, to filter out small animals such as shrimps from mouthfuls of water.

A BIT BATTY

Rhamphorhynchus was one of the first pterosaurs, and had a diamond-shaped rudder at the end of its tail. Its nasty, forward-pointing teeth were perfect for stabbing fish, but it never grew much bigger than a large seagull. It wasn't very well designed for standing upright, and probably roosted hanging upside down like a very big bat!

DINO QUIZ

How big was the horribly-toothy *Rhamphorhyncus*, wingtip to wingtip?

a) 1 metre
b) 2 metres
c) 5 metres

What was *Archaeopteryx*?

a) a dinosaur
b) a reptile
c) a bird

Which living bird has claws like a pterosaur's halfway along its wing?

a) hoatzin chick
b) Australian tickling parrot
c) none of them, silly!

(answers on page 32)

FISH FINGER

The pterosaur's wing bone was actually a very long fourth finger – the other three were very short, probably used for grooming and climbing trees. Since most pterosaur fossils are found in prehistoric sea beds, scientists once thought that those creatures swam about underwater. Now they think they were just dedicated fish-eaters!

Rhamphorhynchus (painted fossil cast)

MONSTERS OF THE DEEP

While dinosaurs ruled the Earth, some reptiles returned to life in the sea. They adapted to hunting many kinds of sea life, from fish, squid and other reptiles to shellfish and other crunchy snacks from the sea bed. Some were truly monstrous!

HERE BE MONSTERS!

Elasmosaurus would have been a scary sight, at up to 13 metres long. It may have held its head above the waves, to surprise any curious fish with a sudden strike from above. Other sea reptiles, such as *Kronosaurus*, had toothy skulls up to twice as big as that of *Tyrannosaurus rex*!

PLUCKY PLESIOSAURS

Some people think that another family of sea reptile, plesiosaurs, might have survived to the present day. Although some plesiosaurs had short necks, many looked very like *Elasmosaurus*. They are the closest thing to the mystery beasts reported today in lakes such as Loch Ness in Scotland.

REPTILE RULES

Because they were reptiles, not fish, sea reptiles had to come to the surface to breathe air. Most also had to clamber onto a beach to lay eggs, just like modern-day sea turtles, but they kept adapting to sea life. *Ichthyosaurus* learned to give birth to live young in the water, and some of its descendants grew special jaws for crushing giant shells.

Elasmosaurus

TURTLEY AMAZING!

Archelon was a giant sea turtle, up to 4 metres long. It lived around 220 million years ago.

YE OLDE DOLPHINNE

Ichthyosaurus was the first complete dinosaur fossil ever found. Two children, Mary Anning and her brother, Joseph, spotted it in Dorset, in 1810. It looked like a very big, streamlined dolphin with a pointy beak.

Ichthyosaurus

DINO QUIZ

How long were a *Liopleurodon's* fangs?

a) 5 cm
b) 8 cm
c) 10 cm

What was unusual about *Opthalmosaurus*?

a) its white coat
b) its big eyes
c) it wore specs

Why did *Cryptolodicus* have ribs around its belly?

a) to keep it nice and slim
b) to support its powerful flippers
c) for squashing crabs

(answers on page 32)

DINO QUIZ

In 1667, an Oxford University professor decided that dino fossils belonged to...

a) demons
b) very large frogs
c) Roman elephants

Why was Georges Cuvier ahead of his time?

a) he was a time-traveller
b) he believed in the idea of extinction
c) he always ate his greens

What is an ammonite?

a) a giant sea snail
b) a sort of shelled squid
c) a super-lobster

(answers on page 32)

WHALE MEAT AGAIN!

Mosasaurus was as big as today's biggest killer whales, and had much pointier teeth!

CROCOSAURUS

Early versions of the crocodile may not have been as big as mosasaurs, but they were still four times bigger than today's monster crocs. *Phobosucus* was the world's first proper crocodile, emerging about 135 million years ago. *Teleosaurus* was another sea-faring croc, with a long, tooth-lined snout.

BARMY BITER

Mosasaurus cruised the seas making a meal of anything it found. Its huge jaws could swing unusually wide, to get its teeth into very meaty prey. But it wasn't fussy; scientists have found several fossils of the heavily-armoured ammonite mollusc with mosasaur tooth-holes crunched through their thick shells!

KILLER CROCS & SUPER LIZARDS

Of all the sea monsters in the dinosaur age, the most horrible to meet looked very much like modern-day crocodiles, only a lot bigger. Some were special sea-going lizards called mosasaurs, which all died out along with the dinosaurs, and some were actually ancestors of modern crocodiles.

LAIRY LIZARD

The mosasaur family were the scariest lizards ever! Apart from their flippers, they looked very much like crocodiles, but they were huge, and very strong swimmers. *Mosasaurus* itself, the big daddy of the mosasaur family, grew up to an astonishing 9 metres long, with jaws the size of a *T-rex*!

Mosasaurus

MONSTER MINE

The first *Mosasaurus* skull was found by astonished Dutch chalk miners in 1770, long before we knew about dinosaurs. Fortunately for science, the skull was looted by Napoleon in 1795, and taken to Paris.

A pioneering French scientist called Georges Cuvier studied it, concluding that it belonged to a giant lizard.

Mosasaurus skull

AWESOME ARMOUR

In such a dangerous world, hefty plant-eaters had to develop a range of special defences to avoid being everyone else's lunch. Sometimes a few spikes were enough to scare their enemies away – but if those didn't work, having a skin that predators would break their teeth on was a big help!

FEARSOME FRILL

Triceratops didn't bother with full body armour. It had a bony frill at the back of its skull which extended over the neck, protecting its spine from a paralysing *T-rex* bite. Mounted on the frill were three huge spikes. If a *T-rex* missed with its first bite, it could find itself impaled on these deadly 1-metre horns.

Triceratops

NICE BUT DIM

Stegosaurus didn't waste its energy daydreaming – it had a brain the size of a walnut.

STING IN THE TAIL

Stegosaurus means 'roofed lizard'. When scientists first found *Stegosaurus* skeletons, they thought the 1-metre-long bony triangles lay flat over its back like roof-tiles, not upright as is now believed. But either way, it certainly had a serious defence – four big spikes in its tail, for swiping at irritating nippers.

Stegosaurus

TANKYLOSAURUS

The most heavily-armoured animal ever to walk the Earth was *Ankylosaurus* (see page 4). Weighing several tonnes, and up to 5 metres long, it grew special bony plates in the skin all along its back. These fused together to form an impenetrable shield, like a tortoise's shell.

NICE TO BEAT YOU

If you saw an ankylosaur wagging its tail, you wouldn't mistake this gesture for a friendly invitation! At the end of its tail, the bony plates in its skin grew into huge clubs, up to a metre across. Under attack, the ankylosaur would lie flat on the ground, letting predators break their teeth on its skin, and giving them the occasional wallop with its skull-shattering club tail.

DINO QUIZ

How did *Ankylosaurus* protect its eyes from attack?

a) with protective goggles
b) it tucked its head in
c) it had bony eyelids

When did *Ankylosaurus* live?

a) 200 million years ago
b) 120 million years ago
c) 70 million years ago

What were *Stegosaurus'* 'roof-tiles' used for, if not armour?

a) toast rack
b) temperature control
c) to show off

(answers on page 32)

DINO QUIZ

How small was the smallest head-banging pachycephalosaur?

a) 2 metres
b) 5 metres
c) 10 metres

What did scientists first think *Parasaurolophus* used its bony crest for?

a) for snorkelling
b) as a means of defence
c) for catching frisbees

What were the balloon-like skin flaps on *Tsintaosaurus'* nose for?

a) to attract a mate
b) to make its call louder
c) to help it hold its breath underwater

(answers on page 32)

FULL SPEED AHEAD!

This car-sized bonce belonged to *Torosaurus*, a relative of *Triceratops*.

NOSEY NEIGHBOURS

Some hadrosaur skulls are riddled with holes. Fossils can't tell us what organs might have existed in these hollows, but some people think that they might have housed extremely sensitive smell receptors. These might have made it possible for hadrosaurs to use scents for communication!

BARGING BONCE

Corythosaurus had a semi-circular bony crest on its head. Scientists think they may have a good idea of what this was for, because there is a living example. The cassowary, a flightless bird in Australasia, uses the crest on its head to barge through undergrowth. At 9 metres long, *Corythosaurus* could have done some serious barging!

Corythosaurus

BONEHEADS

The duck-billed hadrosaur and the crazy cephalosaur families had some of the weirdest skulls in the world. Some had skulls with 25 cm of solid bone on top, while others had amazing tubes running through their heads. Since there is nothing very much like them alive today, scientists can only guess what their curious boneheads were meant to do.

HEAD CASE

Pachycephalosaurs had bizarre dome-shaped heads, sometimes surrounded by a 'crown' of blunt bumps. The dome was formed of solid bone, making the whole head into an extremely heavy weapon, perhaps used as a battering ram. Males might have bashed each other with their heads to win mates, just as goats do today.

Pachycephalosaurs

SECRET WEAPONS

NOSE PICK

Where do you think *Iguanodon's* spike belongs? Gideon Mantell guessed it went on the dinosaur's nose!

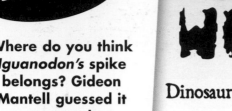

Dinosaurs found some very inventive ways to defend themselves from attackers. If they didn't have thick, armour-like skin or a bony club of a head to protect them, there were still some other tricks they could use.

HEADS OR TAILS?

Since dinosaur skin isn't preserved in fossils, we will never know what colours and patterns dinosaurs were. But some scientists guess that ankylosaurs might have had eye-spots on their club tails. Thinking that it was about to bite the ankylosaur's head, a *T-rex* would get a mouthful of club instead!

Iguanodon self-defence

THUMBS UP

The first dinosaur skeleton to be rebuilt, an *Iguanodon*, was put together by Gideon Mantell in 1835. A spike was found along with the skeleton, and Mantell decided that it belonged on the creature's nose, like a unicorn! Scientists later discovered that the *Iguanodon* had two thumb-spikes which it used to stab would-be predators in the neck.

THE BIG WHIPPER

Giant sauropods, such as *Diplodocus*, had to have long tails to help balance their amazing necks. The thick part of the tail was useful for supporting itself when reaching up into the trees, while the stiff, bony end made a very effective whip to flick at predators.

PESKY PLANTS

Huge herds of hungry herbivores were a real menace to prehistoric plants. Ferns and conifer trees all developed their special poisons and spiky leaves to combat dinosaur diners. When all the dinosaurs suddenly died, these lucky plants were left so well-armed that no other large animals had a chance to evolve ways of eating them.

Diplodocus

DINO QUIZ

What other secret weapon did giant sauropods use?

a) stamping on small predators
b) beastly burps
c) scaly skin

Which present-day reptile squirts blood from its eyes in self-defence?

a) the Tasmanian lizard
b) the horned lizard
c) the cobra lizard

Where are *Ankylosaurus* fossils found?

a) Asia and America
b) Antarctica
c) Australia and India

(answers on page 32)

MUMMYSAURUS

Dinosaurs typically buried their eggs and left their young to fend for themselves. *Maiasaurus* means 'good mother lizard', earning the name after a dinosaur nesting site was unearthed in Montana, USA, in 1978. From clues around the nest site, it was obvious that this large plant-eating dinosaur took great care of its young.

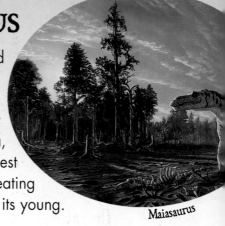

Maiasaurus

DINO QUIZ

How long was the scythe lizard's claw?

a) 50 cm
b) 72 cm
c) 91 cm

Termites first appeared...

a) 220 million years ago
b) 100 million years ago
c) 70 million years ago

How long was a *Maiasaurus* hatchling?

a 35 cm
b) 1 metre
c) 1.5 metres

(answers on page 32)

NICE NEST

Maiasaurs nested in big colonies, as modern sea birds do. From trampled egg shells in the fossilised nest, we can tell that the young maiasaurs stayed in the nest for some time after hatching. The adults would have defended them from small predators, and brought them chewed-up food to eat.

VEGGYSAURUS

Most dinosaurs were, in fact, plant-eaters, roaming the prehistoric landscape in harmless herds. *Iguanodon*, despite its size and its deadly thumb-spikes, only had teeth for snipping twigs from plants and grinding them up.

NOT SO SCARY

Palaeobiologists are people who study the bones of animals to find out how they lived. They can tell from fossils that some dinosaurs weren't at all scary. The teeth are the biggest clue: spiky, sharp teeth are usually for cutting meat; wide, flat molars are more likely to be used for chewing plants.

Therizinosaurus

CLAWFULLY NICE

The biggest ever claw belonged to *Therizinosaurus*, or 'scythe lizard'. You might think that this made it a fierce predator, but its head was small and it had no teeth! The mysterious claw was probably just used for scratching at termite mounds. So *Therizinosaurus* was no more dangerous than a modern anteater.

WHO ARE YOU CALLING CHICKEN?

Some dinosaurs were quite cute – *Compsognathus* was roughly chicken-sized!

MOVIE MONSTERS

Everyone enjoys a good monster story, so dinosaurs are very popular with film-makers. The only problem with making films about dinosaurs is that they were all dead about 65 million years before the first humans walked the Earth. Or were they...?

Scene from Jurassic Park

Scene from The Last Dinosaur

BACK FROM THE DEAD

Film-makers can't hire dinosaurs as extras, so they have to use special effects. Before computers, dinosaur models were built out of clay, and were moved by hand. The alternative was to glue strange frills and bumps onto lizards, and film them in slow motion. *The Lost World* (1960) even used a customised crocodile!

MAN VERSUS MONSTER

The other problem facing dinosaur stories is to explain why there are humans and dinosaurs alive at the same time. The film *One Million Years BC* didn't bother to give a scientific explanation, pitting dinosaurs against cavemen. The 1925 version of *The Lost World* sent explorers to a strange place in the Amazon jungle where dinosaurs had survived.

LOLLYSAURUS

Discoveries of frozen woolly mammoths in the 1970s caused a lot of excitement, and a few films were made on the basis that frozen dinosaurs could be brought back to life. In *The Last Dinosaur* (1977), some unfortunate oil-prospectors in Antarctica accidentally defrosted a *Tyrannosaurus rex*!

NOT SO EXTINCT

In *Jurassic Park*, the dinosaurs were rescued from extinction by gene science, using dinosaur blood found in a fossilised mosquito's stomach! Greedy competitors sabotaged the dinosaur zoo, but not before the scientists had learned some interesting new things about the long-dead reptiles.

FAME AT LAST!

The little dinosaur with the longest name is *Micropachycephalosaurus*.

DINO QUIZ

Where has a 65-million-year-old meteorite crater been discovered?

a) Yucatan, Gulf of Mexico
b) Timbuktu
c) Crater Lake, Oregon

Which of these is a real theory of dinosaur extinction?

a) the dinosaurs were harvested by aliens
b) mice ate all the dinosaurs' eggs
c) the dinosaurs drowned in a flood

Which of the following is the oldest survivor?

a) the turtle
b) the dragonfly
c) the shark

(answers on page 32)

SUDDEN IMPACT!

If a meteorite 10 km wide crashed into the Earth, it would fill the atmosphere with dust, blocking out the Sun, and causing a sudden drop in global temperatures. Large animals would be the first to suffer, but plants and animals of all sizes, even underwater, would be lucky to survive.

Meteorite colliding with the Earth

FOUL FUMERS

Another theory is that volcano activity gradually increased, polluting the atmosphere with gases and ash, blocking out the sun, and causing freak wintery weather. This would explain why some dinosaurs seem to have died out a little while before the mass extinction.

THEY'RE OUT THERE, SOMEWHERE!

Modern birds are probably very close relatives to the last of the dinosaurs.

MORE DANGEROUS THAN DINOS

The sudden extinction of dinosaurs and other creatures 65 million years ago is unexplained. There are all kinds of different theories, but all we really know is that something came along that meant death to all dinosaurs...

NOT DEAD, JUST DIFFERENT!

Not everyone agrees that dinosaurs suddenly died out. Some think that they evolved to meet new environmental conditions, perhaps becoming the first birds. *Archaeopteryx* first appeared around 140 million years ago, with clear signs of fully-developed feathers. Was it a dinosaur, or a bird? Nobody can tell.

DARK STAR

Perhaps the most frightening theory is that our Sun has an unseen partner, nicknamed Nemesis, which passes through the comet belt around our solar system once every 26 million years. Every time it does, thousands of comets tumble out of orbit, bombarding our part of space. Scientists have found evidence for extinctions every 26 million years.

Archaeopteryx

Index

Quiz answers

- **Page 3** a, 80 million years ago; c, a bone that has turned to stone; trick question – there are fossils on every continent.
- **Page 4** c, 675 kg; b, 5 x the length of a chicken's egg; c, 10 metres.
- **Page 7** a, 120–170 million years ago; c, keep eating your popcorn; b, nearly 2 metres.
- **Page 8** a, 140 million years ago; b, they made nests in the hills; c, by the shape of their teeth.
- **Page 11** b, an ostrich; c, 10 times their size; b, fossilised footprints.
- **Page 12** b, 150 million years ago; b, for better grip on prey; a, 1824.
- **Page 15** a, 1 metre; trick question – no one can decide; a, hoatzin chick.

- **Page 17** c, 10 cm; b, its big eyes; b, to support its powerful flippers.
- **Page 18** c, Roman elephants; b, he believed in the idea of extinction; b, a sort of shelled squid.
- **Page 21** c, it had bony eyelids; c, 70 million years ago; b, temperature control.
- **Page 22** a, 2 metres; a, snorkelling; b, to makes its call louder.
- **Page 25** a, stamping on small predators; b, the horned lizard; a, Asia and America.
- **Page 26** c, 91 cm; a, 220 million years ago; a, 35 cm.
- **Page 29** a, 1912; b, microfilm hidden in a dinosaur fossil; b, nuclear explosions.
- **Page 30** a, Yucatan, Gulf of Mexico; b, mice ate all the dinosaurs' eggs; c, the shark.

Acknowledgements

Copyright © 2006 *ticktock* Entertainment Ltd. First published in Great Britain by ticktock Media Ltd.,
Unit 2, Orchard Business Centre, North Farm Road, Tunbridge Wells, Kent TN2 3XF, Great Britain.
All rights reserved. No part of this publication may be reproduced, stored in a retrieval system, or transmitted in any form or by any means electronic, mechanical, photocopying, recording or otherwise, without prior written permission of the copyright owner.
A CIP catalogue record for this book is available from the British Library.
ISBN 1 86007 957 1 Printed in China.
Picture Credits: t = top, b = bottom, c = centre, l = left, r=right, OFC = outside front cover, OBC = outside back cover, IFC = inside front cover
Ann Ronan @ Image Select; 19. Natural History Museum; OFC (main pic), 2/3, 4/5, 5b, 6, 8, 10/11, 13t, 14/15, 16/17, 17, 18/19, 20/21, 22/23, 22, 24, 25, 26/27, 31.
Science Photo library; IFC, 8/9, 12b, 21, 26, 30. The Kobal Collection; 6/7, 11. The Ronald Grant Archive; 28/29.